Ying Chen's Impressions of Summer

translated by

Peter Schulman

Finishing Line Press
Georgetown, Kentucky

Ying Chen's Impressions of Summer

Copyright © 2017 by Peter Schulman
ISBN 978-1-63534-090-7 First Edition
All rights reserved under International and Pan-American Copyright Conventions.
No part of this book may be reproduced in any manner whatsoever without written permission from the publisher, except in the case of brief quotations embodied in critical articles and reviews.

ACKNOWLEDGMENTS

The translator would like to thank the following people for their invaluable help with this project: Muriel Singer, Ying Chen, Patrick Leimgruber

Publisher: Leah Maines

Editor: Christen Kincaid

Cover Art: Peter Schulman

Peter Schulman's Author Photo: Susan Wansink

Ying Chen's Author Photo: Zohar

Cover Design: Elizabeth Maines

Printed in the USA on acid-free paper.
Order online: www.finishinglinepress.com
also available on amazon.com

Author inquiries and mail orders:
Finishing Line Press
P. O. Box 1626
Georgetown, Kentucky 40324
U. S. A.

Table of Contents

Ying Chen's Impressions of Summer 1

Poems (Haiku) by Ying Chen
Preface by Ying Chen
Translated by Peter Schulman

PREFACE

(This is an abridged version of the preface from the original French/Chinese publication)

[…] I am seduced by [the haiku's] potential to tighten life within a narrow moment, into a few words, without thought or even without imagination at times, yet with total engagement of body and spirit. It allows one to experience what surrounds that instance without having to have a narrative. I am no doubt attracted to the familiar, as the haiku that I have read remind me of ancient Chinese poems that adhere to different rules yet share a similar style.

The poems in this collection are inspired by haiku but are free formally and devoid of any spiritual ambitions. […].

For the sake of honesty, I would like to mention that I also embraced haiku writing because I had been devastated by turmoil and several incidents during these last few years.

On the one hand, the premature death of a family member remains a shock that I still can't (or perhaps will never) describe. Something had to change. Something changed. That is what is precisely related to one's perception of things. One can no longer see the world, oneself and everyday life in the same manner. One discovers and rediscovers the immensity of a moment. Simultaneously awake and somnambulistic, I felt as though I were falling through a temporal hole which reminded me of my own disorientation fifteen years ago. It's at that point that one can get closer to a quasi "haiku" state of mind. […]

Haiku can help us to experience an eternity within a moment, to fully embrace, with all our awakened senses, misery along with happiness, displeasure along with pleasure. Everything that happens to us from within and from without, would become an object of contemplation with no priority given to one or the other;

there would be no classifications of any kind. What happens to us in a precise moment would be digested by our senses and would become a part of ourselves, of our children and of what surrounds us eternally.

The majority of the verses in this collection are devoted to my children for whom I die and live.

IMPRESSIONS OF SUMMER

1.

look over there
over there look my mommy
mom look over there

2.

empty balcony
the wind approaches nearby
vehicles passing

3.

a shadow takes leave
rushing to the patio
a crackling dry throat

4.

by evening's return
laughter and tears rushing in
blood and flesh break through

5.

a book lies open
the children playing next door
eye lids almost shut

6.

the lift bridge rises
anticipating a boat
clattering noises

7.

a tic-toc tic-toc
echoing from a blue clock
sheets of white paper

8.

an inert pigeon
lies lifeless on the pavement
established steps

9.

a child is standing
on the edge of a terrace
facing out to sea

10.

little by little
levels of hesitation
a sign of healing

11.

between the light clouds
and the occasional waves
not a boat passes

12.

a cherry pattern
the child plays a game of war
on a tablecloth

13.

sun ignites the beach
someone humming a ditty
seeks a cooling shade

14.

as I am watching
the child is also watching
a moving seashell

15.

such softness is sand
he digs and jumps from the hole
hardness at the core

16.

a local man waits
a beautiful woman sits
a lonely city

17.

shadows from branches
unpredictable pleasures
movements from below

18.

closeness from afar
appearing from the window
distance from up close

19.

within the port's din
passage of day after day
calm houses remain

20.

light rain is falling
every house an island
all else is the sea

21.

a full moon rises
a roaring wave is appeased
the tip of the sea

22.

below a window
the boy and the morning breeze
rocking him to sleep

23.

what a child you are
I am sighing and he says
but what a mother

24.

houses stacked above
the children are playing ball
an expanding sea

25.

Sunday we gather
listening to the ringing
a dominical bell

26.

an evening meal
a familiar rumor
through an unknown street

27.

window by window
one by one lights are kindled
without loneliness

28.

the landscape becomes
children walking on the shore
along the ocean

29.

gone in the morning
they return by nightfall
they come home transformed

30.

peach juice dripping off
juice sliding down an arm sleeve
fingers following

31.

the body is small
a child licks a popsicle
the joy is immense

32.

the bee flies away
depleted from all the fear
a relaxed body

33.

the one who has left
breathing in the child's drawing
among the living

34.

sleeping serenely
on a bench before the sea
as the sun awakes

35.

amidst the beach bags
seen in the elevator
a white orchard stem

36.

the child whispering
within sounds of guns and swords
complete tenderness

37.

a lasting moment
I see within the child's gaze
profound union

38.

noises from the world
the port is a large village
stirring at lunch time

39.

sailboats are racing
daytime waits in the distance
sleeping villagers

40.

delightful chaos
the children's toys are scattered
completing a house

41

radiant morning
nothing seen is nothing felt
life is suspended

42

as dusk approaches
in a pool of black water
a man is fishing

43

today is not here
we don't have a yesterday
only this sea counts

44

evening takes flight
skimming the water's surface
a golden sparrow

45

within the body
an entire universe
a pregnant woman

46

from the speeding cars
a confusing roundabout
swirling dizziness

47

there are two children
rushing with their stooped mother
with very dry skin

48

a blinding light shines
on the watery surface
unbearable hue

49

relaxed on the sand
the sandals of the children
are all one can see

50

screaming and running
waves pursuing each other
laughing and falling

51

The sun is plunging
a vessel comes from afar
it carries a vow

52

fireworks ablaze
prevail momentarily
traces of splendor

53

a child's eyes sparkle
so many times in a day
from simple actions

54

bursts of fireworks
are normal parts of a day
when you are a child

55

a very long bridge
a futile proximity
without union

56

among the red clouds
houses with their balconies
illuminated

57

a reassurance
emanating from the breath
of a sleeping child

58

from a song's title
certainly "I do not mind
a life of nothing"

59

enjoying the beach
they are building a castle
that faces the tide

60

there is a rare peace
amidst a scorched Sunday and
a weary body

61

a stack of dishes
laundry hanging in the sun
this is laziness

62

he marches to sea
with a shovel and bucket
on tiny bare feet

63

colorful make up
streaks along an endless path
walking towards the show

64

the children on stage
my eyes begin to moisten
contemplating us

65

the child imitates
during our evening meal
the cries of seagulls

66

our tranquility
in a balcony corner
a patio chair

67

I see the child's back
with feet and hands in the air
the couch is surreal

68

a peach suddenly
appears to have disappeared
in a fruit basket

69

a housekeeper's gift
flashes from the spotless floor
my heart is at peace

70

joyful kitchen sounds
this is our Sunday morning
the child is whistling

71

ice cream is melting
the child is smacking his lips
coldness in his throat

72

the sea is on fire
the sand is but a furnace
dazzling clarity

73

look he is shouting
astonished that from the sea
there are now some clouds

74

after a hot night
the ocean wind is blowing
towards the smiling child

75

seen from a distance
a slow boat a fishing rod
seagulls in motion

76

Heavy from their sweat
a spiral of children's caps
hanging from a hook

77

an open window
offers a persistent fog
we three to swallow

78

couples on the wharf
shimmer from nocturnal waves
and far away lights

79

in a string of days
many sailboats have rested
beneath my windows

80
from the starless night
scents from the sea accompany
the children's small steps

81

he is still living
each expression from the child
carries his traces

82

focused on drawing
the child is sitting straight at
the sun-drenched table

83

children's voices rise
songs in every direction
at afternoon's end

84

sirens from the boats
arouse our past sensations
in the summer night

85

the seagulls long cries
our saturday afternoons
are our tender skies

86

pearls along the beach
giant and tiny footsteps
plethora of prints

87

a few passersby
herald a time without cars
as they walk slowly

88

the children are near
I feel the wind sun and sand
stroking my body

89

strangely in the sky
a gigantic mound of sand
it is the child's head

90

waves along the coast
mirror fluctuating thoughts
from senseless torments

91

the game has ended
there reigns a beautiful calm
before our mealtime

92

turned back by the sea
he continues the struggle
with his tiny arms

93

rice cooks on the fire
the child is humming his tune
alone in his room

94

the root of a tree
has become two stone faces
metamorphosis

95

abundant sea life
discovered haphazardly
when the tide is low

96

patches of green moss
a richness of brown seaweed
a cluster of shells

97

seagulls are flying
a heron is not moving
ravens are crowing

98

rows of little ducks
floating with their families
call the sea their home

99

on the way to school
the feet and arms of the child
are raised very high

100

it is our Sunday
the bell tells us by striking
that we are alive

Saint-Nazaire, July, 2006
Vancouver, March 2007

Ying Chen's Bio-Bibliography

Born in Shanghai in 1961
French studies from 1979 to 1983 in University of Fudan, and from 1989 to 1991 in McGill University
Living in Vancouver since 2002

Recognitions:

France-Canada prize 1995,
Quebec Librarian prize 1995
Readers' price from *Elle* magazine 1995
Gérard-Moreau Price (British Colombia) 2015

Titled Chevalière en lettres by French ministry of culture 2003

Listed for French Femina prize 1995, IMPAC Dublin Award 2000, Premio Letterario Acerbi 2002, Quebec college prize 2009, Canadian Governor General Award 2015 (catagory essay)

Books published:

The Slow mountains, essay, by Boreal, 2014
Other fantasies, novel, by Boreal and Seuil, 2013
Species, novel, by Boreal and Seuil, 2010
A Child at my door, novel, by Boreal and Seuil, 2008
Summer Impressions, poetry, by Editions Meet, 2007
The Eater, novel, by Boreal and Seuil, 2006
Four thousand steps, essay, by Boreal and Seuil, 2004
Skeleton and its double, novel, by Boreal and Seuil, 2003
Field in the sea, novel, by Boreal and Seuil, 2002
Immobile, novel, by Boreal and Actes-Sud, 1998
Ingratitude, novel, by Lemeac and Actes-Sud, 1995
Chinese letters, novel, by Lemeac and Actes-Sud, 1993
The Memory of water, novel, Lemeac and Actes-Sud, 1992

Dr. Peter Schulman is Professor of French and International Studies at Old Dominion University. He is Chevalier de l'Ordre des Palmes Académiques and the author of *The Sunday of Fiction: The Modern French Eccentric* (Purdue University Press, 2003) as well as *Le Dernier Livre du Siècle* (Romillat, 2001) with Mischa Zabotin. He has edited a critical edition of Jules Verne's *The Begum's Millions* (Wesleyan University Press, 2005) and recently translated Jules Verne's last novel *The Secret of Wilhelm Storitz* (University of Nebraska Press. 2012) as well as a meditation on waves by Marie Darrieussecq, *On Waves* (VVV editions, 2014); *Suburban Beauty* from poet Jacques Reda (VVV editions, 2009) and *Adamah* from Celine Zins (Gival Press, 2010). He is currently co-editor in chief of a new journal of eco-criticism, *Green Humanities* with Josh Weinstein (Virginia Wesleyan College) and has co-edited the following books: *The Marketing of Eros: Performance, Sexuality and Consumer Culture* (Die Blaue Eule, 2003); *Chasing Esther: Jewish Expressions of Cultural Difference* (Kol Katan Press, 2007) and *Rhine Crossings: France and German in Love and War* (SUNY Press, 2004).

www.ingramcontent.com/pod-product-compliance
Lightning Source LLC
LaVergne TN
LVHW041510070426
835507LV00012B/1462